It's in the Cards

It's in the Cards

Poems by

Carolyn Martin

Cover design by Shay Culligan
Author photo by Robert R. Sanders
Cover photo by Aaron Smulktis

ISBN: 978-1-63980-313-2

Kelsay Books
502 South 1040 East, A-119
American Fork, Utah 84003
Kelsaybooks.com

To those who delight in inevitable surprises.

If something is *in the cards,* it is bound to occur,
it is going to happen, or it is inevitable.

—UsingEnglish.com

Acknowledgments

Thanks to the editors of the following journals who believed in these poems enough to publish them, sometimes in a slightly different version.

Anti-Heroin Chic: "Ice Storm"

Bacopa Literary Review: "Warning"

Blue Unicorn: "Untold"

Book of Matches: "Onward"

The Esthetic Apostle: "Snorkeling with Jesus"

Gleam: "Intimations: A Cadralor"

Gyroscope Review: "Teachings from the Hermit, Slug, and Feral Cat"

The Lake: "Not a Pastoral"

The Manhattanville Review: "Waiting for a Bus to the Cloisters"

Nixes Mate Review: "Lessons"

The Opiate: ". . . when you're lost enough to find yourself . . ."

Pensive: "What the Buddha Shared While Gardening in My Backyard"

The Phare: "Before I Remember Sleep"

SHIFT: "The Buddha Walks into a Bar"

Soul Lit: "Five Wives Have Their Say," "It's in the Cards"

Untold Volumes, Feminist Theology Poetry: "Housecleaning,"
  "Jesus Illuminates His Latest Work of Art," "Preparing Jesus for
  Sunday," "The Angel Gabriel Balks"

Contents

It's in the Cards

The self-righteous dead
can't figure out
what went wrong.
No matter what star
they hang around,
Buddhist monks,
Muslim saints,
and Jewish scholars
dance through the clouds.
Not to mention women
at the gate assigning
mansions for eternity.
Why this messed-up state
when they lived firm believing
what the Good Book said?

Meanwhile,
in this New Jerusalem,
Jesus in his silk prayer shawl,
Muhammad in a three-piece suit,
and Buddha in sandals and shorts
play Texas Hold'em
under a blooming apple tree.

Mary passes by
with bread, wine, and koans.
Athena keeps an eye
on counted cards.
And puckish Pan
tunes into NPR's report
from earth below.
Disparate Christian sects
share worship space—
warily, a voice explains—

above the Holy Sepulchre.
Nothing here to shake
a Bodhi tree until,
The keys to this church
are entrusted
to a Muslim family.

The card sharks
catch the spark
in each other's eyes.
Mary claps one hand.
Athena loses count.
Pan turns the volume up
to cover groans
self-righteousness
cannot suppress.

Onward

Sunday morning   and the dishwasher's hum
backgrounds the crows   fine-tuning   in the cherry tree
like Christian soldiers   gearing up   to march off   somewhere
you like that   simile a lot   and plot it   on a pad
with a red pen   that hypes   "Smoke Detectors Save Lives"
it's happening   again   you smile   at the sponge   floating
in the greasy pan   a choir of crows   revives
a dashed-off hymn   sung   by armies ringing   bells
while green eyes   alarm   every room   set to
screech   at any whiff   of argument   all kinds
of saviors   in this raucous world   where details play
ambitious roles   you school   the Keurig   and microwave
they rev you   up   to battle   with a poem   that won't say
where it wants to go   not even to wine glasses   clashing
with coffee cups   or flatware standing   attentively   in the heat

Preparing Jesus for Sunday

Before we go in, let's review the liturgy:
the Gathering/Greeting/Gloria/ Epistle/Gospel/
Sermon/Creed/Consecration/Lord's Prayer/
Sign of Peace/Communion/Collections/Recessional/
coffee and donuts in the hall across the street.
Did I forget anything?

No. Leave your guitar in the trunk.
The folk group played last night. Like I said,
Saturday became a second Sunday years ago.

Woman priests? I wouldn't hold my breath.
I know . . . You were clear: your club included everyone,
but centuries have not been wise. Lying prone on
the church's steps won't change any minds.

Do me a favor: listen to the Gospel carefully.
I'd like to know if you really said what it claims.
And please don't doze during the homily.
No one can best your show on the Mount.
Your rhythms mesmerized and so did . . . but I digress.

At communion time, extend your hands palms up
to receive your body, then move toward the cup
to sip your blood . . . That's not what you meant?
Not literal? For God's sake, that's heresy.
Hold your tongue or they'll sack you before
you can illuminate your take on theology.

On second thought, maybe we should try
the Lutherans down the street. Their woman pastor
is committed to social justice ministries and may need
a guitar for Sunday services next week.

Waiting for a Bus to the Cloisters Museum

New York City, a Sunday in May 1980

She rushes down the brownstone steps
and asks me to zip up her floral dress
since her husband's still asleep and she's late
for brunch with friends whose spouses bore
them to the brink of death she says
as she pulls her hair off her neck so I can trace
the curve of her back past a half-slip's waist
over the bra that defies gravity
to pearls announcing elegance
and I'm embarrassed by a brush
with faultless skin as my nun's short veil tangles
with the wind from buses zipping by
and when she says without judgment
or dismay *You're a rarity* it's true—
a stranger dressed in black appearing
just in time via Providence or Chance—
and she slides into a cab—leaving me
bemused by her epiphany and eager
to contemplate seven storied tapestries.

Lessons

What is Buddha? a young monk asked.
Three pounds of flax, the Master said.

and   if I begged   he might add   cacophonies
of cranky crows   racing south   and squirrels
splooting   in reluctant trees   and mountains
rising decorously   through   mizzling dawns
and the exquisite   Black man   strolling down
grocery aisles   unaware   of my awe
reflecting off   freezer doors   and my teenage date
kissing me   until   my father raged
the porch lights on   and the shade tree   mechanic
down the street   fiddling with   his brakes
to throbs   of Sgt. Pepper   and   his lonely hearts
and everyone/thing   I'll never see   before
this life   spins out   and everyone/thing
waiting   ecstatically   for my rebound

What the Buddha Shared While Gardening in My Backyard

I hate gloves, too. The feel of dirt is bliss.

Consider every weed bodhi-full. It's the nature of Nature.

When the sounds of wind surf through your Douglas firs, stop to hear the rhythms of the universe.

A favorite Rumi verse? *I should sell my tongue and buy a thousand ears.* An art-full deal.

What's my favorite image for rebirth? One flame, many candles. Silence? A raindrop hidden in a gingko leaf. History? A braided river—twisting, weaving, winding through marshes and valleys, over waterfalls—searching for the ocean it calls home.

Don't bring a frantic urgency into your yard. It drowns out mindfulness and agitates the sangha of excellent flying friends.

One gladiola bulb planted mindfully is worth more than a thousand seeds scattered by the wind. Although . . . the wind has a wisdom of its own.

Do no harm to moles and slugs. They have work to do.

After a rain, tread lightly on your lawn. Earthworms are right-sizing in the sun.

Boredom can't exist if you are curious. Become the ripple in a pond searching for its stone of origin.

Uprooting someone's peace of mind is as harmful as uprooting their flowering plum.

Of course, you can read the *Farmer's Almanac* or any garden book, but experience will dictate volumes of your own.

Not a Pastoral

These things/Astonish me beyond words.
—William Carlos Williams, "Pastoral"

Without a rural itch, what I know of sheep
could fill one line. I prefer milkmaids
invested in the Dow, shepherds who own
Victorians in town, and local news
bemoaning the death of malls.

*

When you asked me to take down
the star magnolia tree, I took you literally.
To the ground, I heard, although
I loved its flowering. You yelled,
A trim! too late. We bemoan empty space.

*

Beneath the ragged edge of fall,
leaves lose the lyric tint of cherry, maple, plum.
They'll fossil on lawns and concrete unless
some poet rakes them into a lasting line
like *Letters spelling 'death' are not a death.*

*

We're warned: a frigid sea will crash at dawn.
One day to shut gardens down before icy snow
smothers dahlias, mums, roses, and bamboo.
I'll cut and rake urgency as daylight shivers out.
We're warned: the world is shutting down.

*

It goes with saying—the way a willow's wave
says wind, rain says bounty or flood, fire says
death and rebirth—Earth is uncertain
she will endure. Perplexed by our complacency,
she yearns for the grace of requited reverence.

Leaf Fall

Late autumn and the game rages on.
Six weeks of blowing/raking/recycling
in between foggy frost and rain.
Neighbors tease about whose belong to whom—
cherry/maple/myrtle/star magnolia—
and groan at Nature's outside joke:
as soon as lawns are clear, leaf-devils swirl
dervishly around our cul-de-sac.
We call timeout and plan to reconvene
tomorrow if the sun breaks free.
Which makes me wonder: what if
leaves fell in unison? We could pick
a Saturday before football games kick off,
and gear up to tackle one morning's work
to shut the season down. We'd bench
memories of grudges and gripes and cheer
each other on with splashes of camaraderie.
But . . . a second thought: Nature may be wise
with her leaf-by-leaf strategy.
What if grief came all at once?
Or failure, love, success, crinkled skin?
What if, in one determined day,
we faced decades of experience?
It's the doling out that makes life bearable.
This afternoon, after I store my rake and gloves,
I intend to chat with my star magnolia tree.
Branches of pussy willows are blooming
beneath her dome of half-green leaves.
I'll thank her for nudging me off the couch
when her yellows sprinted down the street
and ask if she can estimate
when the thousands holding on will fall.

I want to strategize how to say good-bye
before we lock our doors, turn our lights
inside out, and hibernate until
buds argue their way into early spring.

Ice Storm

at first   it seemed improbable
we've been duped   before   storm
warnings   fizzle   snow-fears
dissolve   into nothing   much
but this time   ice   upon
ice   upon ice   we groused
God-disturbers that we are
as power lines   sagged   limbs   snapped
heavenly bamboo   prostrated itself   on the ground
during unchosen   cloistering
we recharged phones   in idling cars
and buried food   in the frozen yard
fretted over   feral cats   ground thrush
and anxious squirrels   that disappeared
yet how could we   with our gas fireplace
and stove   complain   when tents and tarps
scattered on   our highways' slopes
couldn't hold   rough sleepers' body   heat
or when we learned   four lives had choked
on poisoned air   eight more died   in nursing homes
after the melt   we'll celebrate   the brutal beauty of ice
for protecting   communities of crocuses
for heaving beds   of warming fir   over jasmine vines
for forcing us   to contemplate   as we stutter-stepped
through the dark   lives beyond   the sliver of our galaxy

Before I Remember Sleep

Most unhappiness comes from not being able to sit quietly in a room.
—Pascal

Tonight, my open window invites in
     the neighbor's front porch lights
          and the frenzied cat courting a reluctant mate.

How Zola pops up at the foot of my bed
     mystifies; but, as soon as he shouts,
          I came to live out loud, Van Gogh saunters in

and shoulders him aside. *What would life be—*
     authority's in his voice—*if we had no courage*
          to attempt anything? Shushing them,

I'm sure they scared the neighbor's friends waving
     their goodbyes and unwound the randy cat.
          Neither rebounds from my complaint before

Wilde flounces across the floor. Waving hands announce,
     Work is the refuge of people
          who have nothing better to do.

He aggravates a red-faced Marx. *History repeats itself,*
     he snaps, *first as tragedy, then as farce.*
          Buddha removes his shoes, finds space

to meditate. Jesus bounces across my bed,
     singing *King of kings and Lord of Lords.*
          A stunned Muhammad blocks his ears,

surveys the crowd, rolls his prophetic eyes.
     I'll wait for the room to breathe collectively.
          Then I'll pontificate, *Doubt nothing and everything.*

Untold

From my front yard,
I watch the truck haul away
his wheelchair, walker, oxygen,
boxes of meds, tubes, and bags.
His wife never told him he was going to die.
The hospice nurse? A home-care aide.
The hospital bed? A necessity
to relieve her back, keep him safe.
And he never told her how Death took up
residence in the reclining chair.
How they'd comfort the cat that seemed confused
and chat—agreeably—about the gifts
of this lifetime, the surprises of the next.
Which reminds me I never shared
my plan to prop my latest poem
against a coffee mug, unhinge
the oven door, mute the pilot light, and sleep.
Death laughed at my fantasy for years.
But today, as the van arrives to pick
the body up, he's standing on the lawn—
alone, grim, reverent. I watch him salute
his latest friend and soothe the cat
lying beneath the maple tree. I'll count
on him to console the wife
as she grasps what "widow" means.

Five Wives Have Their Say

1. Adam's wife complains:

By day he gathers nouns and I zest
them up with verbs and descriptive words,
stirring up a world. But then
one night he tempted me to bed.
I hinted for slow simmering. He missed
the cue, headed straight for boiling.
I couldn't hold my tongue and let him love.
I grabbed a young fig leaf, huffed off
to the apple tree, leaving him half-sprung.
The serpent smirked. God held His breath.

2. Noah's wife declares:

Measure once. Cut twice. He never gets it right.
An ark in his head and he forgets to feed the goats
and wipe his dusty feet. He cannot hear the lost kid's cry
across the desert sands and weeks go by
without so much as *How are you, my wife?*
He takes his meals alone and claims he talks to God.
I watch him wave his arms around, pointing
to cloudless skies. He mutters about decks,
portals, ramps, and joists and how much rain
it takes to float an ark. I never hear a godly voice.

3. Abraham's wife laughs:

What do three strangers know?
My man hasn't done the trick
in all his hundred years.
Every woman understands old leaven
in old dough rises nowhere.

And yet, authority is in their voice,
stars in their eyes. They urge me
to believe there isn't any land too barren
for the Lord to bloom. I'll wait them out
to see what flowers in my empty womb.

4. Goliath's wife swears:

That morning I knew the way a woman knows.
Word crept through the camp they sent a child out.
Stonewashed shirt, puny staff, his puffed-up God
made them laugh—until he took his shot.
Cheating, that's for sure. A hidden stone,
a lucky strike, while my man only heaved one
well-aimed curse. Words in air. Where's the good?
When you see that boy again—no matter where
or when—tell him to beware. I'm a wife
who won't waste time with puny words alone.

5. Job's wife rails:

No way! *Curse God and die?*
My only line reduces me to *just Job's wife.*
Where were *You* when he tore off his clothes
and cut his hair? Where were *You* when those
annoying fools spat platitudes? Who cleaned his sores?
Who stood by when children, household, oxen, sheep
disappeared? How dare You set him on
a hero's pedestal and leave me out.
Here's *my* manuscript: The final draft. Green light
what's mine as mine. Centerstage. My turn.

The Angel Gabriel Balks

Say what? She's not going to buy it.
Another Leda and the Swan or Perseus?
Why another myth? Anyway, I have a slew
of gigs to attend: that woman who wants the devil
off her daughter's back and the blind man
who lost his job weaving rugs. Not to mention
Elizabeth in her sixth month. Doing it the natural way,
Zachary's insufferable. He's so puffed up.
Can't you send one of the feminines
like Mercy, Faith, Sunny, or Purity?
There must be someone on their team
who'd love tackling this virgin stuff.
It's not in my league. Yes, I know
March 25 is next week. Why the rush?
Nine months to Christmas? Is that a new word?
Wait. There's my phone. Leave the script.
I'll let you know after I ponder it.

Warning

When confronted with the limits of the known world,
a 16th-century European cartographer inscribed the warning
"Here Be Dragons" on a small copper globe. Beware: What lies
beyond is unexplored—and perilous.
—Jodi Cobb, "Strange Reflections," *National Geographic,* March 2019

first you need   a mountain   even a mesa
butte   bluff   or high-rise balcony   will do
any height   to widen   your view   of oceans
forests   canyons   streams   car-clogged arteries
joggers   pacing past   mothers strolling
strollers down   leafy suburban streets
then find   the edge   where the sky melts   into
topography   and wait   for flames   four legs
a scaly frame   listen for   roars muting
seagull screams   screeching cars   or voices
quarreling   beyond   your backyard fence
conjure up   St. George   to ward off   your fear
listen and wait   how long   is up to you
if they don't   appear   ease yourself   down
into the world-at-hand   begin to forage   through
cracks   and chinks   and crevices   through slits
and splits   and rifts   be aware   unknowns
find   a way   of sneaking through   like love
and loss   grief and regret   prejudice and hate
beware of perils   lurking nearby   investigate

I should sell my tongue and buy
a thousand ears . . .

—Rumi

If they could translate the language of trees,
a hundred ears would decrypt how maples stood—
confused and terrorized—when humans first appeared.
Roots, limbs, and leaves roared, *Thieves!*
toward sister pines/brother oaks, down deep
into the innocence of fern and moss.
Beware! was all valleys/forests/mountain tops
heard—and all they needed to hear.

If they could decipher flowers' dialects,
two hundred more would fine-tune
a rose-blossom's sigh, the chortles
of wisteria, the rhododendron's multi-delight
when bees lifted pollen and fragrances
toward hummingbirds motoring by.
They'd even pause to ponder the silence
of dandelions pushing through reluctant grass.

If they could rewind their way through waves
of time, three hundred would stand—
respectfully alert—while Jesus wept/
moaned/groaned and called an audible.
Lazarus stumbled from the tomb.
Martha ripped off his death-soaked clothes.
Mary contemplated sparrows singing
ecstatically in an olive tree.

If the final four could modulate themselves,
they would amp up the sighs of experience,
the whispers of the genuine,
the undertones of grace hidden
in gratitude. Then, on cue, they would mute
the raucous arrogance of voices barking
empty words and nestle down in harmony
with stars humming through the galaxy.

Snorkeling with Jesus

Keawakapu Beach, Kihei, Maui

Don't even think of it! Walking on waves
without a paddleboard is embarrassing.
Anyway, we've agreed it's your undercover day.

Over here. Let's settle in the shade of this plumeria.
After years at the Jersey shore, I've learned
a careless burn isn't worth a tan's vanity.

If you hand me your mask, I'll show you how
to stop it fogging up. A drop of Spit® swished
around each lens will clear the visibility.

Wait! Before you put it on, tuck your hair
behind your ears. Don't miss any flighty strands.
You want it tightly sealed so water won't sneak in.

Now fit the snorkel in your mouth and breathe.
Yes . . . it sounds weird and, beneath the waves,
acoustics will be more intense. But focusing

on breath will help you meditate as angels, tangs,
unicorns, butterflies, and—I'm showing off—
humuhumunukunukuapua`as go swimming by.

No, no! Don't put fins on yet. Wait until you're floating
in the waves. See that guy who pulled his on
onshore? Another drunken crab scuttling in reverse.

A wetsuit? Are you kidding me?
Boss Frog's is three miles away and I've checked:
Maui's water is as warm as Galilee's.

You're right. The graying coral is disheartening.
Some fish boycott the reefs and locals blame
chemicals lushing-up golf course greens.

No . . . it's not a good idea to annihilate country clubs.
Tourism would take a hit. Besides, eco-scientists
are working to solve the problem without violence.

One more thing before we head out:
if you should spot a turtle entangled
in fishing line—I cried last week

when several struggled by—clap your hands,
say a prayer, do whatever to set it free.
Beneath the waves, no one will see.

The Buddha Walks into a Bar

and someone shows him where he's quoted
on a sign to the right of the cashier,
to the left of Bacardi, Absolut, and Hennessy.

In a moment of mindfulness, he filters out
smoky noise and reads:

> **Silence the angry man with love.**
> **Silence the miser with generosity.**
> **Silence the liar with truth.**

That's a lot of silencing, he smiles
at the Yankees cap chatting with the business suit.
A Coors Light and Jim Beam freeze mid-sip
at a voice Amaretto smooth, baritone deep.

Perhaps something more concise, he says.
How about: Give, even if you don't have much?

Without a thought, the suit reaches for his wallet.
The fan begins to pass his cap around.
Enlightenment! Buddha claps
and orders sparkling water for the house.

Meanwhile, down the street,
Jesus and his guitar are collecting coins
for derelicts, heretics, and outliers of every sort.

Someone strolling by reports
a weird guy in a weird yellow dress
talking weird talk at the Rising Sun.

Jesus texts Muhammad,
Buddha's at it again.
Meet you there, the Prophet replies,
and rolls up his rug.

By the time they arrive,
Buddha is lotus-positioned on a stool,
teaching the dharma of celebrating
any time with good vibes and softened hearts.

Jesus pokes Muhammad in the ribs
and sighs, *If you can't beat him . . .*

Before the Prophet can reply,
the trim, bearded Christ jumps on the bar,
turning tumblers of Perrier into pink rosé,
multiplying baskets of potato chips.
Muhammad groans and rolls his eyes.

Jesus Prepares to Chat with Muhammad: Medina, 622 A.D.

Remind them. All you can do is be a reminder.
  —Allah to Muhammad (Qur'an 88:17-20)

I'm stymied. What to say? Moses had his tablets,
Noah his ark, and I admit to miracles. But this orphan
kidnapped into prophethood? His: an angel
who dictates poetry that makes his body ache.

Perhaps I'll remind him he walks with those
whose people got it wrong. Mine were a mess.
Take that legalist who cornered me about
the *neighbor* we should love. I put him in his place
with that splendid Samaritan and watched
his righteousness shrink and skulk away.

I admit his thirteen wives—how shall I say?—
are beyond my ken. But his reverence for women?
Distorted as my own. Not to mention other
heresies embraced in our names.
It's enough to send us back into caves
and re-evaluate why we came.

I'll recap Allah's command to ask
every tribe, here and heretofore,
Where are you going with your life?—
and remind him what Buddha says: everyone
is chosen, no matter the belief or path.

Perhaps I'll close with a vision to ease
his mind: when he's washed earth from his feet,
he'll stroll around Paradise. Joseph has a many-colored coat
he wants to show-and-tell, and Jonah—the whale
smell's worn off—wants to shake his hand.
And, if he's so inclined, there's a daily poker game
under the apple tree. Buddha and I will deal him in.
I'll remind him to bring his rug and latest poetry.

Teachings from the Hermit, Slug, and Feral Cat

—With thanks to Alicia Ostriker's *The Blessing of the Old Woman, the Tulip, and the Dog*

1.
To be alive
says the hermit
is to feel
the cave ooze moss
and my skin
thistle-green.

To be alive
says the slug
is to hide
beneath Hosta leaves
believing no cruelty
will uncover me.

To be alive
says the feral cat
is to wait
at the sliding door
until her coffee cup's half-full
and she readies my bowl.

2.
To be awake
says the hermit
is to hear the evening breeze
chant vespers
through cracked stone
and modulate each verse.

To be awake
says the slug
is to curl beneath
a flower pot
until the gardener
passes by. Relief.

To be awake
says the feral cat
is to find the softest dirt.
Squat, deposit
dinner's residue,
then scratch a lid on it.

3.
To be at peace
says the hermit
is to homeschool
the demons
who are the outside-
in of me.

To be at peace
says the slug
is to rest through
sunburnt days and revel
in the crunching
music of the night.

To be at peace
says the feral cat
is to find
a catbird seat
while squirrels squabble
with Steller's jays.

4.
To be wise
says the hermit
is to recognize
dreams chase me
and beg for a wish
on starless nights.

To be wise
says the slug
is to understand
there's more to me
than slime trails
around my yard.

To be wise
says the feral cat
is to understand
the vacant bowl yesterday
does not predicate
abandonment today.

Housecleaning

When resistance is gone, so are the demons.
—Milarepa

Thanks to that plucky holy man,
I'm happy to report they are packing up.
I filched his trick: invite them to live in harmony.
Without spikes of adrenaline, boredom did them in.
Where will you go? I'm curious.
Anywhere, they laugh, *humans are.*
They ask to leave some stuff behind:
a ratty robe, unwashed plates, piles
of unopened mail, volumes
of explosive rants, files
of rejection slips, narratives
I've acted out for years.
On second thought, I try. *Feel free to stay
until you clean your relics out.*
They roll their eyes—resisting
my naïveté—and suggest
I lock the doors and meditate.

Playing Texas Hold'em Beneath the Apple Tree

Truth is the same always. Whoever ponders it will get the same
answer. Buddha got it . . . Jesus got it. Muhammad got it.
                    —Swami Satchidananda, *The Yoga Sutras*

The most excellent jihad is the conquest of one's self,
Muhammad says as he scans the clouded sky.
Agreed, Buddha replies. *Better to conquer yourself*
than win a thousand fights.

The Prophet grins relief. No Muslim Angel today,
no demands to recite poetry. Just hanging out
in the appled air, sharing one-liners for eternity.
The greatest wealth is the richness of the soul,

he sighs—comfortably pleased. *And riches arrive,*
Buddha's offering, *with a contented mind*
not a bunch of worldly things. They high-five
themselves and wonder what's agitating Christ.

For God's sake, hold your tongues,
Jesus complains. *Focus your contented minds*
on one more hand before the sun decides to set.
Sleep beneath an apple tree is wealth enough for me.

Anything worth doing, Buddha shuffles the deck,
blossoms from the heart. Muhammad can't resist,
Be kind. It beautifies. Jesus glares, *Deal!*
Branches bow. The first evening star smiles.

Nudging Jesus to Get Help

Come on now! It's obvious. You're depressed.
Back in the day, your guys said you wept
when disappointments overwhelmed.
This week you're at it again.

Believe me, I understand. Who wouldn't cry
when polar bears are starving on ice floes
and children line cages in border towns?
It's hard to accept you're not responsible.
God knows you tried to save us from ourselves,
but humans with their flawed free wills do
what humans do. It's time to save yourself.

Maybe a Buddhist or Muslim therapist or,
a last resort, an atheist? You need
someone free from fossilized beliefs
about who you are and what you tried to teach.
Let's Google mental health practitioners.
The town is filled with them . . . But wait . . .

How about I round some children up?
We have several in the neighborhood:
Vietnamese, Ethiopian, a few mixed families.
We'll invite them to sit at your feet
and you can entertain with lilies of the field,
sparrows, and mustard seeds.
Throw in a few miracles—like how
you walked on water to calm your antsy crew
or busted Lazarus out of his tomb.
Play up the angle of the walking dead
and how he smelled when his clothes fell off.
Kids like that kind of gross and will take it literally.

Be sure to add how heaven is here—
although I'd chuck any *kingdom* metaphors.
Focus their unclouded eyes on the glory
of a slug, a feral cat, a gingko tree.
Teach them how they're connected
each to each and earth's their fragile playing field.

If you resurrect your innate charm,
I bet these innocents will check the validity
of your beard and heal your cracking heart.

Jesus Illuminates His Latest Work of Art

With all due respect, I call it "The Boss's Dinner."
We'd hang out in this upper room frequently
to debrief and strategize. When a rocky boat
is heading toward a risky shore, my guys craved
assurances that, steering it, I knew the way.

The round table is one my father carved.
Each time I laid my hands on it,
I felt the flow of his quiet strength.
Behind the scenes, he taught me well.

The beauty on my right? My dearest Magdalene.
Her job: updates on women working on our team.
How tending to the poor and sick, loving those unlike
themselves, they spread our good news efficiently.
My men—threatened by her confidence—
could barely nod, confirming, I regret, some
lessons will take centuries to stick.

On my left: Judas, my good friend.
Get this straight: he only did what I asked.
He begged me to promote someone else,
but I convinced him he was up for it.
It pains me I never saw how it would end.
Call it, if you will, the "Judas Principle":
a cautionary tale for leaders everywhere.

The profiles centerstage are Matthew and Mark
arguing about their narratives. They seemed
to care more about applause than truth.
A seat away, Luke rolls his doctor's eyes.

From stage right, my favorite young mystic
carries unleavened bread he baked before
the sun agreed to set. Stage left, that's Peter
with a bag of figs, James with a sack of fish.
The other five? Hidden in the wings somewhere
with flasks of wine nicked from a wedding feast.

I wish I could say that the white space was intentional—
like psalmists settling silence in their songs
or scribes margins on their scrolls—but that would be a fib.
God-honest-truth? My brushes were wearing down,
my pigments drying up, my time running out.
Sometimes good enough is all that is.

It tickles me you hung it in your dining room.
I love the way morning sun haloes the scene
and afternoon shade invites a closer look.
And it chokes me up to see it lit by candlelight
as you break bread, sip wine with family.

Intimations: A Cadralor

1. *Don't praise the day before sunset.*
                    —A Polish saying

But what about the choir of crows warming up
at 5 a.m.? They deserve praise and so do parents
falling out of bed bone-sore, spilling lives
in factories and cubicles. And so do kids
trekking to school with homework almost done.
And so do teachers raising shades in students' eyes.

2. *One should lie empty, open, choiceless as a beach—*
waiting for a gift from the sea.
                    —Anne Morrow Lindbergh

Evening fog softens an angry reef of clouds.
Pretentious crows scavenge torn crab claws,
dead starfish, and mussel shells on the messy shore.
A single gull reflects on a wave-made pool.
You head home in your sand-scattered shoes
with one impressive oyster shell to paint words on.

3. *Summer afternoon . . . to me those have always been*
the two most beautiful words in the English language.
                    —Henry James

The dusty baseball field vanishes beneath
a circus tent, crews of clowns/jugglers/acrobats,
smells of generators' exhaust and animal heat.
Trade-off: August games for kettle corn
and tickets to cheap seats to watch
the practiced surety of tightrope and trapeze.

4. *The ear is the only true writer . . .*
                    —Robert Frost

When eyes turn down, ears tune up:
sirens, horns, quibblings on the street;
hallway voices ignoring "Quiet Please"
when they pass the hospice door.
The last words he whispers: a request
you record the sound print of his final breaths.

5. *I enjoy the spring more than the autumn now.*
One does, I think, as one gets older.
                    —Virginia Woolf

Too soon, the calendar says, for bleeding hearts
and daffodils, crocuses and squills. Yet, here
they are risking late frost to illuminate
your eighth decade. You praise them for proving
death's impermanence and tell the brisk blue sky:
Never too late old, never too soon wise.

. . . if you're lost enough to find yourself . . .

—Robert Frost, "Directive"

Before we knew pollution was a word,
we played beneath yellow skies. Down the road
belching oil stacks didn't seem troubling.
Nor did the miracles of DDT,
plastic bottles and bags, or gas-guzzlers
testifying to white-picket dreams.
We snubbed the signs in hurricanes, fires,
and droughts. Discounted leaded paint and pipes.
Muted the whimpering of bees. Ignorance
had a way of keeping closed eyes tight. Now
decades almost-too-late, we gasp at miscues,
at the arrogance that hurled us toward
the brink. *Enough,* we shout in churches,
meeting halls, and schools. And if *enough*
should lead to *find,* we'll beg to recalibrate.
We'll celebrate each mizzling dawn
when blue nibbles through unwrinkled gray
so mountains can come out. We'll bless each stream
that braids its way to and from its ocean home
and embrace each tree that holds our rootedness.
We'll pray that sheaves of poetry will rise
from rewilding fields where tigers romp
with elephants, lions with antelope.
If Earth accepts our belated reverence,
we'll find our way to a new paradise.
By day we'll dance—waggishly naked and wild—
through orchards, forests, and fields of daffodils.
By night we'll fly across the sky like free-
floating rogues searching for righteous stars.

About the Author

From associate professor of English to management trainer to retiree, Carolyn Martin is a lover of gardening and snorkeling, feral cats and backyard birds, poetry and photography. After decades of writing academic papers and business books, she finally realized that poetry is the way her mind interacts most creatively with the world—in images, rhythms, sounds, and intensities of language. Consequently, for the past fifteen years, she's settled into the joyful challenge of translating experience into as few words as possible. Her aesthetic is embodied in Jack Kerouac's comment in *Dharma Bums:* "One day I will find the right words, and they will be simple"; and in Galway Kinnell's statement, "To me, poetry is somebody standing up . . . and saying, with as little concealment as possible, what it is for him or her to be on earth at this moment." Her poems attempt to be simple in words as they grapple with the complexity of being on this planet at this time.

Carolyn's poems have appeared in more than 175 publications throughout North America, Australia, and the UK. Her fifth collection, *The Catalog of Small Contentments,* was published in 2021 by The Poetry Box. She currently serves as the book review editor for the Oregon Poetry Association. For more, see www.carolynmartinpoet.com.

www.ingramcontent.com/pod-product-compliance
Lightning Source LLC
Chambersburg PA
CBHW071113090426
42737CB00013B/2590